Down to Earth
Spirituality

Christian Personhood
Global Concerns

Down to Earth Spirituality

Albert J. Fritsch, S.J.

Photographs by
Warren Brunner

Justo L. González

Sheed & Ward

Global Concern

Scriptural quotations are taken from The Jerusalem Bible, Darton, Longman & Todd, Ltd. and Doubleday & Company Inc., Garden City, New York, 1966 (with inclusive language modifications).

Sheed & Ward™ is a service of National Catholic Reporter Publishing Company, Inc.

Library of Congress Cataloguing in progress.

ISBN: 1-55612-468-6

Published by: Sheed & Ward
           115 E. Armour Blvd.
           P.O. Box 419492
           Kansas City, MO 64141-6492

To order, call: (800) 333-7373

Contents

Acknowledgements

We would like to thank Sharme Price for spending so much time and effort finding the right photo for each of the reflections. Without her efforts this book could not have been possible. Likewise, we owe a great debt of gratitude to Robyn Arnold, who supplied the technical and editing assistance to make this project successful. Thanks to both of you.

Dedicated to the Down to Earth

"Then I saw a new heaven and a new earth."
(Revelation 21:1)

            a   *a*   *a*

Down-to-Earthers find it necessary to burrow in deeper and deeper. Hopefully you already have a dedication to the Earth but, perhaps need to cultivate it further. This series of social and psychological ecoanalyses and reflections is meant to be your spade and is awaiting your honing and use.

A good Earth tool cannot afford to be cumbersome— and so with this book. Every word saved increases its versatility. The tone is deliberately sobering because Earth-saving is such. We need time to reflect—precious time to recapture our well-being and niche in the environmental landscape. And to do so we must be clear and alert. Thus we dedicate this book to you its readers, who are willing to use it and improve the Earth by so doing. May we always remain grounded in this Earth and love it as a Mother.

INTRODUCTION

Divergent Paths

*"The one who rose higher than all the
heavens to fill all things is none other
than the one who descended."* (Ephesians 4:10)

❧　　　　　❧　　　　　❧

Our environmental crisis is not in failing to know but failing to do. It's easy to say "Let's cease talking and start acting" or "Roll up your sleeves and do something." What is needed is both a reflection on the method to bring about a proper action and the will-power to carry it out. Let's give as much attention to strengthening that will-power as to finding out environmental degradation details.

"Down to Earth" is a way of acting because our planet is in trouble and we have to do something about it. We can't afford to go up to the stars, or out to gurus, or leave it to the experts. It's unreal to deny that forests are being destroyed and land eroded. If we get our hands dirty, let's do more than busy work, which gives a sense of false accomplishment, but wastes our most precious resource, our time. We have a few fleeting moments of life; let's make every moment count.

Action

Appreciate the microorganisms which flourish in the soil around us. They are necessary to life on this planet. Make a compost pile and add organic materials such as kitchen or garden wastes. Protect it, turn it over, spread it when it is ready for use. Talk compost to others.

Denial

"God made every kind of wild beast, every kind of cattle, and every kind of land reptile. God saw that it was good." (Genesis 1:25)

ða   ða   ða

All created things are good. This primary Scriptural and theological fact refutes the ancient Middle East belief that there were good and bad portions of creation. Instead, this eternal truth tells of our persistent human tendency to deny the goodness of portions of creation. But we can easily misinterpret the Biblical message. Some optimists among us deny the environmental problem because good so overwhelms them. "Environmental pollution can't be that bad." Others of us say creation is to be used for our own particular purposes. For these, consuming resources is part of their divine mission to hasten the Day of the Lord and the end of Earth as we know it. Will Judgment Day find us still messing up this Earth?

Action

1. Make a list of all the creatures which you appreciate and recognize as good.

2. Stop when you are tired and admit that it is a far longer listing than you have time to record.

3. Now, give some extra attention to your own pets.

Escape

"Always consider the other person to be better than yourself, so that nobody thinks of one's own interests first but everyone thinks of other people's interests instead." (Philippians 2:4)

჻   ჻   ჻

We run from environmental concerns through consumer spending, fast boats, drugs, alcohol, television, or one of many allurements and distractions of our modern culture. We escape the deteriorating world by retreating into temperature-controlled buildings and manicured lawns and barriered yard spaces and choose not to look beyond. We take up our time in frivolity, becoming survivalists seeking to remove ourselves from the impending dangers to the Earth. We wrap ourselves in our own self-interest. We are the Earth's great escapists.

Action

How many luxuries are around the house? How many are truly needed and how many do we fool ourselves into thinking we need? How about giving away one luxury this year?

Excuses

"You know how to interpret the face of the earth and the sky. How is it you do not know how to interpret these times?" (Luke 12:56)

ﺿ   ﺿ   ﺿ

We acknowledge an environmental crisis but find it too difficult to face. We leave the matter to the experts—and ignore the invitation to become democratic in environmental problem-solving. We may be victims of over-institutionalism, overspecialization, and over-watching of professionals on television or movies. Others of us are armchair quarterbacks. Through false humility many excuse ourselves as too lacking or too dignified. We have no training in this field, union card, or financial resources.

The challenge for us is to appreciate our talents and opportunities and still recognize limitations. No other age has been called to save the Earth or, in fact, has realized the Earth could be destroyed through human mismanagement—or saved through good management. The call is a momentous but humbling one. I might not be able to save this Earth but WE can.

Action

Go through this month without ever saying "I can't do that." Resolve to do something you thought was beyond your own current practical expertise. Tell it to another. Share this sense of achievement with others.

No Time to Daydream

"Why are you standing here looking into the sky?" (Acts 1:11a)

&a;   &a;   &a;

Let's discern the most realistic environmental actions which apply to ourselves and our communities. Answers are not up in the stars, but down here on Earth, not given by a uniquely-insightful or respected person, but in the democratic process of all of us being participants. We can't afford to daydream, to drift into the future or step backward in history hoping to reach the good old days. Let's plant our feet firmly on the ground and eyes on the path. Celestial speculation, even billion-dollar ventures into space travel, star wars and space stations waste our resources better spent on saving planet Earth. We must get on with earthly tasks. Times are too urgent to dally. Our past gives clues but not answers; our future gives hints, but has to be created. When we dream, let's construct a realistic one—that all creatures have enough to eat and decent places to live.

Action

Do something about the suffering of the world. Don't let crisis fatigue overwhelm you. Others need our surplus and our individual support. Help someone start a garden this year.

Keep Our Bearings

"The wise one sees ahead,
the fool walks in the dark." (Ecclesiastes 1:14)

ᴥ   ᴥ   ᴥ

We can't live in the macro- or the microcosmos. We are tempted to investigate the infinite worlds of outer space and its evolutionary paths, or an infinite microcosm below our feet with its own complex structures. We stand at the point between these infinite worlds, a finite stance within our own particular bioregion. It's the here and now, not the there and then. If we lose our bearing and forget our direction, we grope, stumble and make costly mistakes. Let's know our exact place and direction. The "now" is fully living the year's seasons and the "here" is our particular locality. Concrete and asphalt paving separate us from the "here" of our habitat; artificial lighting from the "now". In its most essential feature, being down-to-Earth is an awareness of our place (home) and our time (*kairos*).

Action

Do a household audit of any harmful chemicals which might be present. Many chemicals are unneeded or stored improperly. Resolve to rid the home of such contaminants. Think about converting your home to a commercial chemical-free zone.

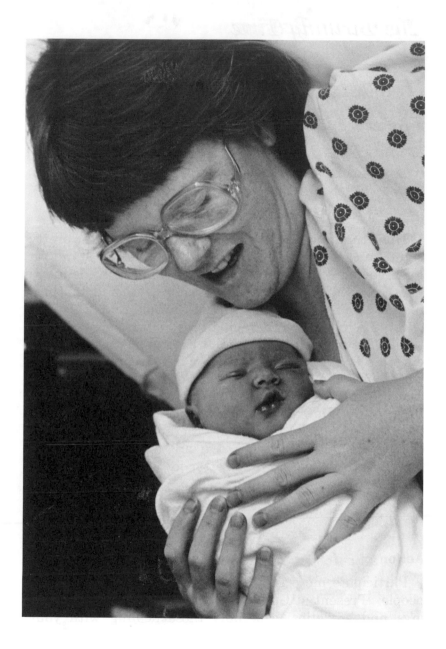

The Birthing Time

"From the beginning till now the entire creation, as we know, has been groaning in one great act of giving birth." (Romans 8:22)

❧   ❧   ❧

Unfortunately the "here and now" is not a pretty sight, thus the temptation to escape. Who can stand for long gazing at devastated Earth, fouled air, denuded hills, eroded land, spoiled waterways and natural places? Being in tune with Earth means that we suffer with this planet's other creatures, which are in pain until a New Earth is born. But contrary to some prophets, this is not yet a New Age or new creation; it is the time before the completed birth event—a birthing time— and those that frolic have abandoned the painful birthing process. Down-to-Earthers can make the vital difference, giving special attention, time and effort to making the desecrated holy again. We are to prepare for the birth of a New Earth. Far better for us to be midwives than premature celebrators.

Action

Participate more fully in the liturgy as a work of the people. Present at God's altar your own concerns, sufferings and anxieties, especially those dealing with your everyday life.

Being Uniquely Ourselves

"I will make you the light of the nations so that my salvation will reach to the ends of the earth." (Isaiah 49:6b)

By being "Down-to-Earth," we—

—control our striving for mastery of other creatures,

—understand our community with all beings,

—use resources with responsibility,

—hear the cry of the Earth and respond,

—join in the community of sufferers,

—teach others to do the same,

—speak out clearly when others are hesitant,

—celebrate small victories,

—and wisely choose those actions each can do in his or her given time and place.

Action

Make an environmental retreat and discover (maybe with another) where you are drawn to help at this moment.

First Principle: Connectedness with Creator and Creatures

"Praised be my Lord for our mother the earth, which does sustain us and keep us, and brings forth divers fruits, and flowers of many colors, and grass." (St. Francis, "Song of the Sun")

      ʔꙮ   ʔꙮ   ʔꙮ

By touching and being close to Earth we feel the connectedness which actually exists, our nearness to our relative, our mother Earth, who gives us birth and life. By molding and working the Earth we learn from her and permit other creatures to be our teachers. Down-to-Earth indicates the direction we turn for fostering growth. As the plant turns to the sun, we turn down to Earth, bending before our teacher and showing our respect and appreciation for what the Earth can give. If we are learners seeking wisdom, we soon see Earth as primary teacher—without denying the role of books and thinkers. Getting out of touch with the Earth is due in part to external social, political and economic pressures. Through proper social analyses we understand the influences which damage Earth and how we have been so complacent and unmoved.

Action

Read or reread some basic ecology to understand the interconnection of all beings. If you are beyond this stage of learning, delve into a nature book in a currently unfamiliar area.

Second Principle:
Our Action Requires Sacrifice

"God, create a clean heart in me, put into me a new and constant spirit, do not banish me from your presence, do not deprive me of your holy spirit." (Psalm 51:10-11)

ঽঌ   ঽঌ   ঽঌ

Being in touch with Earth gives us a sense of nearness and compassion, of head and heart. Earth teaches us more than descriptions of plants, animals, seasons, wind, and ocean currents. We acquire Earth sensitivities, not mere factual knowledge. Those who love Earth vibrate with it, enter into the passion of Earth, seek forgiveness for transgressions done to our Earth, and (at the risk of being anthropocentric) declare environmental degradation to be a major crime against humanity—and against the Earth and all creation itself. Harming Earth damages our human relationships and communities. After Nuremberg we can't stand idly by when crimes against humanity are committed. Creatures, as teachers, direct us to help our suffering neighbors and to spend our time wisely.

Action

Begin to keep a listing of things to be done for the coming month. At the end of the time period, see whether these things have been achieved. Accept other preempted needs as a good reason, if that be the case. Don't let failures depress you.

Third Principle: Our Action Is One of Complementarity In Which Many Gifts and Talents Are Called Forth

"Tell them that they are to do good, and be rich in good works, to be generous and willing to share." (I Timothy 6:18)

❧   ❧   ❧

Clashing polar opposites are from a bygone Newtonian and Hegelian age. Ours should be an age of complementarity, of making opposites interact with each other, of accepting the dynamics of diverse but meaningful lifestyles, philosophies, spiritualities, and methodologies. Greater vitality comes through interaction than from fighting. Teamwork is ennobling: being willing to accept mistakes as part of learning, thinking like people with limited resources, and encouraging others to act.

If Earth were for us an elaborate, highly-pristine artwork or goddess, then we wouldn't act or dare touch it. On the other hand, if we see our Earth in familiar terms or as mother, we become ourselves doing Earth-renewing teamwork. We rebuild our habitats and feed ourselves. We are confident enough to do almost anything, propelled into a self-reliant, democratic, environmental process, exercising different talents in a complex community. We become forerunners of a new healthy ecosystem, which respects and fosters diversity.

Action

Volunteer to help in a community project this year in some special way. Become a team member at least for a day. It does not have to be a competitive exercise.

An Overview

"Do not disappoint us; treat us gently, as you yourself are gentle and very merciful." (Daniel 3:42)

≈   ≈   ≈

"Environmentalist" is a neutral term, for all of us reach out and touch our surroundings and affect them in some manner—either for good or bad. Maybe we've over-used the term and salve our consciences by superficial environmentalism, like driving a gas guzzler 10 miles with a small bundle of recyclables, or contributing to an environmental group with directors making six-digit salaries. Being a good environmentalist is more than discussing acid rain over cocktails or signing petitions.

Action

Let's go beyond our current environmentalism and—

- Rediscover our personal relationships with the Earth;
- Examine the subtle social pressures restraining us;
- Find poor Earth and poor people as one community of need;
- Recognize the urgency to set priorities;
- Establish the various models of environmental action; and
- Resolve personally to act.

I.
REDISCOVERING
OUR EARTH LINKS

Rediscovering Our Earth Links

"Mountains and hills will break into joyful cries before you and all the trees of the countryside clap their hands." (Isaiah 55:12b)

֍   ֍   ֍

Do we know where we are or what season it is? Do we enter into the liturgical rhythm of the year, the mood swings of our lives? Can we relate to and interact with our Earth, our home, our history? Do we have a superior attitude over Earth's creatures? Is our encounter with creatures fulfilling and joyful? What is our "here-and-now," and how dowe create our home place or environment and our history or moment on this Earth?

We need a phenomenology of our current stance before the Earth's creatures. Earth helps give us our bearings. For nothing is more disconcerting than losing our sense of direction or not knowing what day or time it is. Knowing place and time allows us to help create our own life, our environment, our home, our era, our age, our portion of history.

Action

Purchase or check out library books pertaining to the local bioregion and learn about the geology, native plants and animals, cultural history, and the economic geography of where you live. Start your own mini-library of such materials.

Creature Teachers: Ole Nellie

"If you would learn more, ask the cattle, seek information from the birds of the air. The creeping things of earth will give you lessons, and the fish of the sea will tell you all. There is not one such creature but will know this state of things is all of God's own making." (Job 12:7-9)

ﻙ   ﻙ   ﻙ

Our cows went to back pastures to have calves. One stormy summer evening I had to find and bring home the newborn calf. Sure enough, it was in the most remote and secluded spot on the farm, and the storm was only a half-hour away. How could I, a 14-year-old, carry that calf a half-mile? I was about to give up when the cow nudged me gently and I went ahead. She followed and the calf trailed behind. I hurried and so did she, a footstep behind, and we beat the storm to the barn by minutes. My lesson learned from Ole Nellie was: become a leader by not pushing and shoving from behind; lead by going up front. In all my dairy years, that event was never repeated, but that cow-taught lesson lasted.

Action

Consider what your own spirit creature is, the one with which you identify more easily and feel somewhat personally related. Learn all you can about the habits and practices of that creature. An alternative exercise is to write down and describe how one or other creature has taught you a profound lesson.

The Glory of Creatures

"The fig tree is forming its first figs and the
blooming vines give out their fragrance."
(The Song of Songs 2:13a)

 ❧   ❧   ❧

We are born into a glory-filled environment, born to
make it ever more glorious. The wonder-filled journey of
childhood includes the discovery of nice things: flowers, but-
terflies, cobwebs, and frogs, colored leaves in autumn and
snowflakes in winter. It's also a world of fleas and briars
and icy paths and frost-killed flowers. Nature's glory and its
harder side have an appeal and teach us reality, the
changes of life, the meaning of life and death, a need to
respect the stinging and prickly creatures. Often creatures
teach us individually, but more often it is by observing
them in their life cycle and their interrelationships with
other creatures that we start to see better our past and future, our niche in a balanced environment.

Standing on the banks of the crystal Merced River as it
flows through Yosemite National Park, it seems miles removed from cabins and park roads, though only a hundred
yards away. But a quarter-million visitors each year leave
their mark even on this pristine stream. So do the forces of
ever-changing nature and recent fire storms. We are
tempted to ask whether there really is untouched nature, or
is it imagined? Have we made it more glorious or do we
disfigure our planet/classroom?

Action

Occasionally pick up litter in a public place and dispose of
it properly. Granted, you do not litter, but why wait for some
maintenance crew or authority to remedy the messy situation?
In some ways, litter is the responsibility of all of us.

What About Power?

*"They are like grass sprouting and flowering
in the morning, withered and dry before
dusk.—our life lasts for seventy years, eighty
with good health."* (Psalm 90: 5b-6, 10)

ᎧᎧᎧᎧᎧᎧᎧᎧᎧᎧᎧᎧᎧᎧᎧᎧᎧᎧ   ᎧᎧᎧᎧᎧᎧ   ᎧᎧᎧᎧᎧ

We recognize both our power and powerlessness. We are at a fine point, a convergence of two rays, one streaming to us from the Creator and the other from our community of fellow creatures. While that point defines where we are (our place and time), we are sometimes confused and disoriented about our HERE and NOW. Earth and the community of creatures give place and character to us—and say who we are by where we are. We cannot bilocate. We are here at a given site, at a specific time, at the close of the second millennium A.D.

The Earth is our mother, our origin, our cradle, our grave, our anchor, our mirror giving us the first glimpse of what we are. Earth tells us that we are neither small nor large, just ourselves. Getting down-to-Earth keeps us aware both of the greatness of our surrounding creation and the limits of our own being. If we know where we are, we know a little more who we are and why we are.

Action

Share already-known or newly-acquired information about your natural location/area or bioregion with a younger person who wants to learn. If you need to embellish the narrative, consider further reading and research.

Building Sand Castles

*"With heaven my throne and earth my foot-
stool, what house could you build me, what
place could you make for my rest? All of this
was made by my hand and all of this is
mine—it is Yahweh who speaks."* (Isaiah 66:1-2a)

    ꝫ   ꝫ   ꝫ

Earthly creatures teach us that we can have a home if
we create it properly and preserve it, once created. However, many feel unable to care for themselves, are told
they are worthless and on a grand dole. Their overly-institutionalized lives drain them of self-respect and this,
in turn, leads to a loss of respect for others and Earth
itself. Creativity evaporates and powerlessness prevails.
Pathetic people say "I have never constructed anything,
or touched the soil in a meaningful fashion, except to
make mud pies or sand castles on a beach." Granted,
mud pies and sand castles have recreational value. But
they don't relieve world hunger or homelessness.

Action

Either help others to build or refurbish their home or
build something yourself with or without others. It may
be a small shed, a tree house, a lean-to, a basement
room. If this is a new experience, don't hesitate to seek
advice from skilled construction people.

The Homeless

"The sparrow has found its home at last, the swallow a nest for its young." (Psalm 84:3a)

ﾞﾞﾞ   ﾞﾞﾞ   ﾞﾞﾞ

Rapid mobility makes many find it difficult to identify with a given place. Pity those with no place to call home. Our home place near Washington, Kentucky was within sight of my father's home place and just out of sight of my mother's family farm. That gave our family a sense of locality. But our case is not the ordinary, for one-fifth of the nation's people moves every year. No wonder census-takers have problems. Those sad songs about leaving home or being far away vie with others about never having a home. Birds have nests and foxes dens. We need abodes which are more than past memories or future dreams. Let these be places of familiarity and belonging, proper dwelling and food-growing space. Home can spring up in our nation's vacant lots and plots. Granted, we risk embarrassing mistakes in home-building and gardening, but in the end it is a priceless home.

Action

Give support to those who care for or have a ministry to undocumented workers or Central American refugees. Can you help identify facilities which may serve as sanctuaries for those fleeing political harassment in their own homeland?

Becoming Ourselves

"Think of the flowers; they never have to spin
or weave; yet, I assure you, not even Solomon
in all his regalia was robed like one of these."
(Luke 12:27)

      ಜಿ   ಜಿ   ಜಿ

Performing down-to-Earth work gives us a sense of confidence. We can build our own home, produce our food, surround the living space with proper vegetation, invite in wildlife of every kind, and make the landscape alive. Stories of immense cosmological events or great human feats only paralyze the overly-institutionalized, unspecialized, urbanized. Why dazzle people already too dazzled? Are we worse than other creatures in being keenly aware of our insignificance, miserable beings tempted to a feral, competing life, focused only on survival? Or can we find meaning in the ants, birds and wasps confidently building their respective abodes?

Action

Adorn your surroundings with flowers this year, either within your vegetable garden, as potted houseplants, in a special place in the yard, or in a public place where others encourage and appreciate your own floral contributions.

Recognizing our Blessings

*"You have crowned them with glory
and splendor . . ."* (Psalm 8:5b)

       è   *è*   *è*

Healthy Earth-consciousness is recognizing that we are blessed creatures because of what God has done for us. True humility is recognizing that we are what we are through another—not ourselves. It does not focus on our smallness in a mean, cold, vast universe. Rather we are clothed in warmth, greenery, love, and care, and called to do great things, namely, enter into the very creative process.

The Earth energizes us to do great things, for it becomes the substratum of our cocreativity, the catalyst of our becoming self-reliant. When we touch Earth gently and with respect, it responds and shows us our connectedness with self and our family of creatures. We are more aware of place, i.e., the names of plants and animals, where the river flows, the winds blow, the storms arise. We become attuned to our bioregion, gain self-confidence by using native materials, live more wholesomely off of the land, and we realize our special and unique responsibilities as cocreators.

Action

Organize and develop an annual campout which includes people who do not get opportunities to enjoy the great outdoors. Make the conditions suitable to the type of persons so the stress or fear of natural things will not distract them from having a good time.

Experiencing the Earth

"There is always hope for a tree: when felled, it can start its life again; its shoots continue to sprout. Its roots may be decayed in the earth, its stump withering in the soil, but let it scent the water, and it buds, and puts out branches like a plant new set." (Job 14: 7-9)

❧　　　　　❧　　　　　❧

The Earth beckons and calls us to hear, smell, taste, see. Let's never go to a new place without tasting the land's fruit, root, herb, berry or nut. That's part of our Earth-communion, our openness, love, respect and compassion. We draw from Earth, an inexhaustible teacher: its creatures, the plants and animals and even the geological forms of the Earth itself—springs, mountains and rock formations. All become heralds of our minds which are moving through the passageways of our awakened senses.

Listening to the Earth is an acquired skill. It takes some effort and quality time, requiring us to turn off appliances, radio, automobile, the created noises which fracture contemplation and silence. Earth sounds are different, for they become part of nature's symphony, relaxing and soothing our frayed nerves. Many with perfect hearing never listen. They may go through an entire year without being aware of crickets or songbirds. Human-made noises overwhelm them and they become the Earth-deaf ones.

Action

Besides annual outdoor events, make a resolution to get outdoors daily, if possible. A nature walk is more than just good exercise. It keeps us in tune with the creatures around us and the ones which heal us by their presence.

Morning Song: Beginning Time

"My heart is ready, God
—I mean to sing and play.
Awake, my muse,
awake, lyre and harp,
I mean to wake the Dawn!" (Psalm 108:1-2)

       ಶ   ಶ   ಶ

Rise with the sun.
Inhale fresh air if it's around
Thank God for giving a new day.
It is new life no matter
if it's a crisp and cold day
or a scorcher,
it's cloudy or bright.

We create the day glorious
in our minds and lives
and for those around us.
We insert glory into the
eternal seasonal cycles,
making them our time.

Day follows night and night follows day,
Rhythmic yet with fitful starts and finishes,
punctuated by sunrises and sunsets.
Night is dying / resting time.
Day is rising / living time
—the springtime of the day span.
Glorious morning has broken,
life begins again
on tuned-in Earth.

Action

Greet the new day by uttering a morning thanksgiving prayer for surviving the night and being willing to tackle the challenges this day will bring. It is time for a new start.

Natural Haunts: Beginning Place

"I will plant it on the high mountain of Is-
rael. It will sprout branches and bear fruit,
and become a noble cedar. Every kind of bird
will live beneath it, every winged creature rest
in the shade of its branches." (Ezekiel 17:23)

؏ ؏ ؏

If morning is beginning time, should ideal places be sought as well? Should we start our attunement in a mortally-wounded spot, say a trash heap or eroded field or unreclaimed strip mine site? No, for it's too distracting. Let's begin where Earth is undamaged, its anguish is muted and songs of joy are still heard. Attempting to contemplate while immersed in a severely-wounded patch of Earth is like reacquainting ourselves with a family member in an intensive care unit. Go first to healthy family members and through them enter the arena of the suffering. So also let Earth's beginning place be where Earth's health and vigor is better sensed.

Action

Select and visit your favorite natural reflection spot and see that the place is tidy, has a comfortable resting area, and is ensured of not being damaged in any manner through careless people. Continue to give it ongoing protection.

Touching the Earth

"How often have I longed to gather your children, as a hen gathers her chicks under her wings, and you refused!" (Matthew 23:37b)

ċ   ċ   ċ

Being down-to-Earth deepens our sensitivity to insignificant activities others regard as foolish, e.g., prostrating and kissing Earth, hugging trees, touching flowers, petting dogs. Some we do; some we don't or look hurriedly around to see if others are observing. We communicate with other creatures in our tender touches so that they can respond. Earth energy streams through our bodies with each contact. Some groups naturally make this contact more than others: farmers, gardeners, foresters, cattle herders, nature lovers and wilderness dwellers. These, often but not always, accept Earth-teacher in their own way. Why can't everyone? The challenge we have is to offer all, especially urban dwellers, the opportunities to touch nature in some meaningful way. That is why we are creating our Environmental Trail Program for inner-city youth.

Some shy away and find creatures too insignificant, not worthy of our touch. All creatures need sensing, even if they frighten us awhile. Learning by sensing the Earth is not a competitive game, a graded system. We do so freely by overcoming our initial fears or unfamiliarity with certain creatures. We need to find that position between being overawed for Earth as Gaia, the goddess, calling for obeisance and adoration, and having no respect and seeing creatures as objects of our subjection and conquest. Somewhere in between, fear gives way to gentle respect.

Action

Till or add compost to soil, either in your garden or indoor pots. Make it a habit to periodically cultivate and enhance soil. If such opportunities are remote, look for ways to tend a community garden.

Recognizing Interdependence

"You must not muzzle an ox when it is treading out the corn." (Deuteronomy 25:4)

ॐ   ॐ   ॐ

Most earth-related spiritualities emphasize the harmony between human beings and other creatures. We are interdependent; we exist in an environment in which our mutual health keeps each other alive. It is in our own self-interest to keep other creatures from becoming extinct, even granting this is a rather imperfect motive. In becoming aware of our interdependence, we are only a short step from defending animal rights, caring for stray dogs, rejecting animal experimentation, and championing bird and wildlife sanctuaries.

In discovering interdependence with other creatures, we become more aware of the need to work together to save our Earth. In seeing others' gifts, we find our own. The self-reliance of the wild becomes the textbook for human community self-reliance. Building my house transforms into constructing OUR habitat. Through cooperative endeavor community is remade, the quality of life deepens, and our communities provide their food, water, fuel, and building materials from nearby sources. In so doing, we reduce our drain on the Earth's resources and make this a cleaner and better place to live. Ironically we discover our human interdependence through self-reliant action—in Earth community.

Action

Read about threatened animal and plant species and voice your concern when a good opportunity arises, such as a letter to your Congressperson. Provide nesting areas for wildlife, if this is within your power.

Sustaining Enthusiasm
(translated, "The God Within")

"And know that I am with you always; yes, to the end of time." (Matthew 28:20b)

    ❧   ❧   ❧

I once paused in my jogging and listened for a long time to a singing mockingbird. All its song seemed so wasted because others were not listening. Was this magnificent treasure of sound all for me? Good creatures like mockingbirds abound. They inspire us to new ways to organize our experience, gather data, work with materials, communicate, and expect response. We become alive with the sound of Earth Music. It effervesces and fills our atmosphere with joy. We can become overwhelmed, distracted, risking the loss of the moment of creative opportunity. The Good News is that the Earth gently teaches us to sense simple things as conduits to our Creator. Creatures, tabernacles of mystery, invigorate us, beckon us to change, draw us to adoration. Creative enthusiasm can be expressed not only on our knees but as enthusiastic builders of cold frames and composting toilets. That is being down-to-Earth.

Action

Pause in your outdoor work and listen to the sounds of nature. You don't have to try to record them except in your mind's ear. They are God's gift to us. Now, continue to work with growing vigor.

Knowing Limitations

"You modelled me, remember, as clay is modelled, and would you reduce me now to dust?"
(Job 10:9)

Earth's hard knocks awaken us to our limitations. A hill slips behind our house; termites attack the handiwork; drought and bugs ravage the garden; acid rain spoils cistern catchments; clouds hover over the solar panels. Some events and mishaps are due to natural circumstances, some result from our inability to deal with natural forces, and some are caused by outside culprits. Whatever the source, we are limited in our response, since as human beings we're part of something we didn't start. While finding our creative powers, we sense our limitations and failures to attain goals and dreams, and we start to die when we start to live. We are earthbound; we just don't always know it.

Action

Review with another person one of your practical projects which is postponed or has failed. Most people have many examples. Could the barriers be overcome and the project started up again? Who can help jump those hurdles and allow completion?

Champion Simplicity

"Happy the gentle: they shall have the earth for their heritage." (Matthew 5:4)

❧   ❧   ❧

A "Down-to-Earth" spirituality encourages us to be gentle and inherit our place with other creatures. The wasteful are not Earth community people. They have not yet learned or have forgotten how to use sparingly, refuse what will harm, and save some for a rainy day. Strangely, ground squirrels and nesting birds offer lessons to learn. Becoming more gentle as the Earth is gentle is easier said than done, because our modern culture does not pride itself in a conservation ethic. The lack of such an ethic threatens us now and could destroy the gentle teaching community of creatures as well. Will gentleness get a hearing? Will there be an inheritance left?

Action

Audit your own use of resources. Keep tab on the amount of electricity used in one month. Where is conservation of this and other resources possible?

Moving Forward

*"Do horses gallop on rocks, do men plough
the sea with oxen, for you to change justice
into poison, and the fruit of integrity into
wormwood?"* (Amos 6:12)

❧ ❧ ❧

Most reflections on environmental concerns seem over-
whelming and tend to scatter our attention, because
everything is interrelated—and everything is interesting.
Shadows loom. Where is the necessary rigor which
focuses and sharpens our sensitivity to plants and animals? One answer is to couple the relaxed atmosphere of
Earth's classroom with a somewhat-disciplined social
analysis of the current conditions in which we find the
Earth. We want to move from a consciousness of other
creatures to that of human failure in interrelating with
Earth and other people. We uncover and attempt to
tackle social sin. Harsh as it sounds, it must be done.

Action

Help create a resource center of serious environmental
literature. It's best to do this in a place where others can
share the materials, such as in a parish, school or community center library.

II. Analyzing Social Structures

Analyzing Social Structures

"But your mother is covered with shame, disgraced is the woman who bore you; she is the least of nations now; a wilderness, a parched land, a desert." (Jeremiah 50:12)

≈   ≈   ≈

Our social and economic system is in trouble and some say in decline. Whether we can understand it, patch it up, or develop an alternative requires that we analyze what we've got and where we are heading. Being down-to-Earth means knowing the abounding injustices, what causes them, and how we can trigger the healing process. When soil erodes through human negligence, rivers become filled with debris, fish life is disturbed, severe flooding results, and the entire microclimate is changed, there are ecological reasons. When people suffer from lack of food or adequate housing in a land of enormous waste and S & L macroscandals, there are social and political reasons. Spirituality goes beyond personal brokenness and treats social sin, that brokenness of a social structure of which we are part.

Action

Construct a possible scenario of a community examination of conscience which can apply to the institution in which you work or where you pray or have social contact. Ask a trusted friend about its feasibility.

Start Questioning the Circumstances

*"You are the ones who destroy the vineyard
and conceal what you have stolen from the
poor. By what right do you crush my people
and grind the faces of the poor?"* (Isaiah 3:14b-15a)

❧   ❧   ❧

Social analysis requires honesty and a commitment to truth. We see eroded National Forest Land and sincerely ask why. We discover it's done by the off-road vehicles. Why are these allowed? They aren't, but trails are unpoliced and perfectly inviting to those with powerful machines. For what purpose are such paths maintained? To make a trail useable and to provide roads for logging—subsidized at taxpayers' expense, but nonetheless used as is part of the philosophy of the mother agency—the U.S. Department of Agriculture. The forestlands are croplands, recreation lands, not primarily an unused resource. Does logging on government land compete with private tree growers? Yes, but look at the jobs, often for the poor, who have limited employment opportunities in these rural areas. And on and on—the endless tangle of complexity demanding answers which may or may not be rational.

Action

Read about destruction of forest lands, both in this country and overseas. While trees are renewable, are our forests? Resolve to help save the remaining old growth woodlands and to support those helping to protect our endangered forests.

Silent Witnesses

"Pardon me, thou bleeding piece of Earth, that I am meek and gentle with these butchers."
(Shakespeare)

❧ ❧ ❧

If we are down-to-Earth, we'll expose the unjust power structures which deface the planet. Are these structures sinister? Greedy? Hungry for control? Suicidal? Addictive? Idolatrous (placing autos on a showroom dais to be adored)? All or some of the above? The weaknesses are evident, but the causes are more difficult to find. Surely we must come to terms for greed is addressed differently than addiction.

Silence is no cure for crimes against the Earth. Recently, at least 14 cars passed a wounded person in clear view of the public on an interstate near here. People would not dare to get involved. Is that what our silence is like? We aren't willing to know what causes the harm for fear we may have to do something about it.

Action:

Initiate a discussion of when quietness is a needed virtue and when silence is a grave offense against others. Both quiet time and spoken time are needed in our broken world. Exactly when is each required?

Hidden and Subtle

"Everything that is now covered will be uncovered, and everything now hidden will be made clear." (Luke 12:2)

સર   સર   સર

Social analysis is a discipline requiring reflection. It takes a critical mind and critical time to discover and understand the hidden influences of our consumer culture. Often even intelligent folks hesitate to undertake social analysis. Rather, they tolerate a naive understanding of environmental degradation. We read thoughtful criticism of Earth Day-20 celebrations (April 1990) for allowing big chemical and oil companies to help fund the event. How else can you explain the overemphasis on individual environmental responsibility and next to none on social or corporate responsibility? Who controls resources, uses them at will, and in the largest quantities?

Action

Take time to personally examine whether we blame ourselves for things that others cause. Do we overlook our silence to halt social abuse? Ask for God's and the Earth's forgiveness.

Recycling: A Cover-up?

*"You have wrapped yourself in a cloud too
thick for prayer to pierce. You have reduced
us to rubbish, to the scourings of the nations."*
(Lamentations 3:44-45)

           ☙   ☙   ☙

Recycling is a necessity going beyond mere voluntary action. It is now being required by an extravagant and wasteful society. Recycling is a litmus test for growing consumer environmental consciousness. Many know that it's important to return waste materials to production and short-circuit landfills. Fine and dandy. We know that to recycle means conserving resources (e.g., trees, top soil, water). Recycling expends some resources and it may be misused as well as used, namely as a license for further resource expenditure and a justification for future consumer waste. However, many recyclable products shouldn't have been produced in the first place. Returning a used product to wasteful consumption might be a relative saving when it substitutes for virgin materials, but it's still waste.

Social analysis allows us to see recycling in perspective. It is good to some degree, but who pushes it, and why are they wanting us to take personal responsibility? Is it because they find it too costly to substitute goods or processes? Maybe they don't want us to know how useless the item is.

Action

Resolve to recycle one added waste product, but to see the practice as less perfect than not using the material in the first place.

The Small Bottler's Lesson

"When there came a traveller to stay, the rich man refused to take one of his own flock or herd to provide for the wayfarer who had come to him. Instead he took the poor man's lamb and prepared it for his guest." (II Samuel 12:4)

ૐ   ૐ   ૐ

Two decades ago, a small-scale Pennsylvania beverage bottler told us how he could continue profitably using returnable containers in competition with larger-scale producers, provided there was a bottle law. His small business did not find the reusing of bottles anything extraordinary. He had analyzed the pressures behind his industry and found the growing popularity of disposable bottles came from the large-scale centralized bottlers who wanted none of the expense of long-distance empty bottles' reshipment. Switching from glass to plastic lowered their transportation costs, and transferred costs of hauling and disposal to consumers and government under the guise of convenience. Their methods were perfectly logical, perfectly cost-effective, but they were forcing the smaller bottlers out of business. His firm has since ceased to exist.

Action

Use returnable containers where and when possible.

Power Behind Power

"You remember that, when you were pagans, whenever you felt irresistibly drawn, it was towards dumb idols?" (I Corinthians 12:2)

      ஜ   ஜ   ஜ

The driving force behind overconsumption is not consumer greed; it's overproduction. The consumer product industry wants this consumption and wants customers to return soon for more. So advertising is no accident. This advertising pressure is the grease that makes the consumer economy function. We're taught to "need" everything from toys to appliances to automobiles. Advertising creates false insecurities. Peer pressure, the mirage of gadget happiness, sexuality, and the lure of convenience are at work as well. From toddlers nagging mom for a particular cereal placed on the lower store shelves (for their convenience) to the elderly poor in the dollar store, the pressure is for everything from cradle to gravestone. Haven't we been taught this by at least three full years of television ads in an average lifetime? Billboards entice us, radios and loudspeakers beckon us. We're drawn to ever-earlier Christmas rushes.

Wait a minute, a lot of us want it—not so different from the idols of old. Why are the pulpits silent? Is it because many have grown to like it and want more? And they pay the preachers to tell them what they want to hear. Are the healers likewise addicted? Don't the producers fuel the economy? Don't advertising profits fund our institutions? Producers are to blame—and so are we.

Action

Spend less time idle shopping, paging through advertisements, and watching television commercials. Ask your parish leadership for a sermon or homily dealing with excessive consumerism.

Social Analysis and Packaging

"Take the fig tree as a parable: as soon as its twigs grow supple and its leaves come out, you know that summer is near." (Mark 13:28)

❧   ❧   ❧

Disposable beverage containers constitute over 10% of the domestic waste stream, a hefty volume. Excess packaging, as with beverages, takes more resources than do the package's contents. However, a dozen states have drastically changed this through returnable bottle legislation. Large beverage producers continue to fight to keep the remaining states unregulated. Whether litter is beverage containers or other forms of packaging, we know what massive amounts of materials are used. Container waste products tripled in volume in the U.S. between 1960 and 1985. We're up to our necks in resource-draining overpackaging, of boxes within boxes. How much of this is because of supermarkets with fewer clerks and greater need for safeguards against petty theft in unpoliced store aisles? What about producers who want no returnables to disturb their profits? What about the jobs created in the packaging industry, which is largely dependent on oil-based plastics?

Action

Resolve to organize or attend an ecotage party to trash polluters in their manicured front yards.

Using Less is Better
and Living Better on Less

"Every time someone says something about the local conditions, the coal company hires a revival preacher." (Social justice worker in Harlan County, Kentucky)

ða   ða   ða

"Keep America Beautiful," an industry creation, has an American Indian with a tear in his eye. Truly, the pervasive litter is worth a cry, but is the message that personal irresponsibility is totally to blame? The United States alone consumes so much that it depletes the world of the resources needed to handle its appetite. We now approach 50% aluminum can recycling. That means we are adding over 10 billion cans a year to a saturated landscape because the rest are not being picked up. And next year, if we up our collection a few percentage points, we will have almost the same number of uncollected billions. There are other ways, such as mandatory deposits; give them a chance.

Action

If you are in a state with a mandatory deposit law, write friends in another state and tell its advantages; if your state is without such legislation, obtain information about the success in the states with existing laws.

Green Products and Social Reflection

"For if they use the green wood like this, what will happen when it is dry?" (Luke 23:31)

    ea   ea   ea

A proper social, economic, and environmental analysis of many products will find some so-called "green products" (less environmentally harmful than some of their counterparts) to be long-term resource wasters. Why is the recycled paper cup a good product when it signifies a wasteful procedure? If we are going to put "green seals" or "green crosses" on products, first break the consumer addiction, lest these products feed on the impulse to buy more and more.

Doesn't social analysis come to terms with this addiction and how one must go about treating it? Owning up to our condition is the beginning. Changing our ways is a second step. Bringing our coffee cups is better than using one or other disposable variety. But going cold turkey in our addictive disposable culture is not easy. It never is.

Action

Always carry along your own shopping bag.

Natural Versus Synthetic Fibers

"She sets her hands to the distaff, her fingers grasp the spindle." (Proverbs 31:19)

In complex lifestyles, no answer is simple unless we choose to use less. Cotton is good to wear. It looks fine, absorbs well, and has that soft touch, but is it a perfect fiber? Is not a major portion of agricultural pesticides used in cotton production? That means contaminated soil and waterways in vast stretches of the American South and West. Granting the added expense of mechanized farming and manufacture, a thorough environmental audit shows cotton production's environmental impact is greater than that of some synthetic substitutes. Much depends on the added factors of lifetime, resources needed in cleaning and maintaining, disposal problems, expense in processing and refining, amount of technology needed to process materials, and comparative weight.

Granted, some natural fibers have good qualities, such as forbidden hemp. In the late 1930s, DuPont put pressure on government regulators to ban hemp production (for drug reasons) in order to salvage their budding synthetic industry. Except when overseas markets were cut off during World War II, this ban has continued. However, hemp is very versatile, the oil from seeds and the pressed cake is of value, and the crop is very hardy and requires no pesticides.

Action

Determine which fabric is best suited for the article you need to purchase. Then buy according to need, not fashion.

Fuel to Burn

"Give us some of your oil: our lamps are going out." (Matthew 25:8)

ꙮ ꙮ ꙮ

Much of petroleum consumption is for fueling motor vehicles. The public transport systems which served many cities so well in the early part of this century, such as the Los Angeles area, were deliberately dismantled under the pressure of an alliance of big oil companies and the automotive and trucking industries. My parents had far better access to railroads and public transport in rural areas 60 years ago than do we who live in these areas today. They spoke nostalgically of riding the local train in their rural hamlets. That is not possible in most of rural America today—a land devoid of public transportation.

Consumption policy is also dictated by amounts of fuel required to operate the nation's automotive fleet. While it is technologically possible to manufacture cars that get as much as 100 miles to a gallon, we will still not put teeth into fuel efficiency regulations. Cars of as low as 15 or less miles to a gallon are allowed to be produced—if people care to pay the fuel prices. But is that enough? Why should such precious and limited resources be used for those who have the money to waste? Can't efficiency be required?

Action

Carpool whenever possible. Do you need to make this next trip, or can you combine it with another? Check your car for tune-up, proper tire inflation, and overall mileage per gallon.

Chemical Dependency

"Yes, as you have drunk on my holy mountain, so will all the nations drink unsparingly; they will drink, and drink deep, and will be as if they had never been." (Obadiah 7:16)

    ❧   ❧   ❧

We get hooked on chemicals, a nation drugged on pesticides and chemical fertilizers, food additives and multipurpose cleaners. We preach anti-drug messages, send some to prison, and pay enforcers millions to find and hunt out individual culprits. Okay, so far? But what about the big ones, the manufacturers of millions of tons of hazardous materials produced each year, the manufacturers who have hooked a whole nation and world on the need for farms to grow crops with chemicals? And even the land is hooked in turn. Has the campaign extended to them? Has any chemical manufacturer ever spent time in prison for producing a hazardous pesticide? Hypocrisy in drug matters runs terribly deep.

Action

Replace chemical pesticides with less harmful alternatives. If need be, read about and obtain alternatives. Organic farming and gardening associations are rapidly expanding into all parts of America.

Deeper Systematic Questions

"Woe to those who call evil good, and good evil, who substitute darkness for light and light for darkness, who substitute bitter for sweet and sweet for bitter." (Isaiah 5:20)

❧   ❧   ❧

If we are cocreators of the Earth, does this earth-shaking imperative mean anything when the richer one-third of the Earth squanders the resources of future generations? Ironically, the pressure for consumers to keep the pipelines open will be countered by the guerrillas taking hostages and closing down this fragile and vulnerable system. The have-nots are becoming aware of a power based on disrupting a fragile and vulnerable system, just as they have power in their numbers. Why heed pleas about overpopulation when others overconsume? Were the Czech Velvet revolutionaries of '89 forerunners to First World critics and revolutionaries? Are we free enough to conduct a Green Revolution of such a magnitude, and what would the results be?

Action

Get your church to adopt (send support for) a destitute child or family in a Third World country.

Debunking Corporate Power

"I will remove the heart of stone from their bodies and give them a heart of flesh instead."
(Ezekiel 11:19)

❧   ❧   ❧

Are consumer product profit-makers inherently anti-environmental? There is a good case for it. They use vast resources and encourage mountains of waste. They have the power to buy legislators, finance elections, capture governments, and change laws at will. They have mowed down half the planet's tropical forests in four decades and will destroy the rest in another two without sufficient safeguards. They espouse greed in all its forms and make it a virtue.

But not enough has been said and too little provision has been made for what must be done. To make changes, agents need to be human—not tolerating evil and not being forced to love corporate persons as we do human ones. In fact, while we become more human, let's expose the corporate creations for their inherent lack of personhood. Then we can begin.

Action

Partake in boycotts of products from corporations with bad environmental practices.

Factors in Conducting a Social Analysis

"And what I say to you I say to all: Stay awake!" (Mark 13:37)

❧ ❧ ❧

1. An immediate critique of what is promised and what is delivered. If benefits accrue to very few, then the promises have not been met.

2. Assumptions (biases) and contradictions that underlie the object of study. If some say that they favor all the people, but believe in enhancing the prestige and power of a few, then what is said about rights and promises is not being upheld.

3. A satisfactory analysis includes enough facts to act correctly, cutting away distracting and tangential matters, and a wide variety of models to support one's efforts.

4. A willingness to carry out necessary reforms which may emerge, even if it means challenging established patterns of behavior which protect vested power interests.

Action

Join or form a small "base community" and spend some time in discussing these factors.

III. Setting Deeper Roots

Setting Deeper Roots

"Look, I am going to send my messenger to prepare a way before me." (Malachi 3:1)

ೞ ೞ ೞ

Environmental movement people are certain of the righteousness of their cause—and many soon detect this. Do they really perceive what others miss, or isn't this ecofundamentalism? Are some "saved" through their knowledge and others damned by ignorance and misdeed? Or is the descent to the Earth outside of this judgmental mode altogether?

A down-to-Earther lives on another track. The dividing line is not between the arrived and the wayward, but all are to some degree setting deeper roots. Being down-to-Earth involves becoming more rooted, exerting ourselves, not resting on laurels. Our sweaty work is a sacred reality, the nourishment and moisture required to make a New Earth. It involves the basic belief that we can save the Earth and renew it, but this can only be done by our collective efforts. Setting people into opposing camps only delays the process.

Action

Resist vocally any talk about having a superior consciousness about the Earth. Gently caution against Earth fundamentalism.

Some Earth Facts

*"To Yahweh belong the earth and all it holds,
the world and all who live in it; founding it
on the ocean, basing it firmly on the nether
sea."* (Psalm 24:1-2)

     ð   ð   ð

—The Earth is fragile and subject to damage.
—The Earth is suffering through environmental
    degradation.
—This is caused by human misdeeds.
—We are quite capable of both building up and
    tearing down.
—The damage is becoming so severe that the very
    life on this planet is threatened.
—Individually and collectively we must take
    responsibility for this harm to the Earth.
—Part of the blame is our failure to stop the
    culprits from continuing to damage the Earth.

Action

Go out and observe some of the damage to the Earth.
You won't have to go far. Document on film the damage
done. Report misdeeds to the proper authorities and to
the media.

The Mystery of Suffering

"This is why the country is in mourning, and all who live in it pine away, even the wild animals and the birds of heaven; the fish of the sea themselves are perishing." (Hosea 4:3)

❧   ❧   ❧

Just as we enter into creation's mystery through birth, so we enter Earth's suffering by realizing our faults. And this entrance is into a deeper mystery. If one doubts that the Earth suffers, get them to read any environmental exposé. Down-to-Earth people acknowledge this suffering and are willing to become compassionate—or sufferers with the Earth. We are becoming aware that part of this mystery is that the Earth has had to suffer so as to enter into its glory. Therefore, we need to be willing to suffer as midwives to a New Earth.

Action

Improve the earth around you this month in a particular way, such as by cleaning up a pile of rubbish, refurbishing a room, or pruning trees.

A Litany of Earth's Woes

"Wasted lie the fields, the fallow is in mourning. For the corn has been laid waste, the wine fails, the fresh oil dries up." (Joel 1:10)

       ❧   ❧   ❧

—Continuing spills of oil on waterways and the oceans which seem to occur with greater frequency because of oil tanker traffic;

—Cutting and burning of the tropical rain forests and consequent destruction of the habitats of many of the species of migratory birds and other creatures. Some estimate the extinction of one-fifth of the Earth's species by the year 2005;

—Increasing amounts of acid-producing emission products from fossil fuel-burning electrical generation facilities and the consequent production of acid rain and its effects on fragile forests, lakes and aquatic life;

—Erosion of soil through modern agricultural cultivation methods;

—Use of synthetic organic pesticides and herbicides on our land and leaching of these materials into ground and surface water;

—Contamination of indoor air by a variety of chemicals;

—Toxic and solid waste dumping and failure to reduce the generation of harmful waste materials;

—The depletion of the upper atmosphere's ozone layer by chlorofluorocarbons (CFCs) and other emission products.

Action

Set down your own list and prioritize local and global environmental threats.

Poor Earth, Poor People

"Woe to those who add house to house and join field to field until everywhere belongs to them and they are the sole inhabitants of the land."
(Isaiah 5:8)

&a.   &a.   &a.

Down-to-Earth spirituality is not like entering a cool pool inch-by-inch; rather, urgency presses us to take the plunge into deeper and deeper depths of environmental consciousness. Through social analysis we realize that Earth's problems are not removed from human ones. There is an existing community among the poor—poor Earth and poor people. We are not standing solely on the side of a social ecology which concentrates on the injustices to people (poor people), nor on the side of a deep ecology that champions other ignored creatures (poor creatures) as having some equal status with human beings. Let's stand up for both: poor Earth and poor people, and declare that an injustice to one is an injustice to the other. We are not anthropocentric or geocentric, but "paupercentric."

Action

Touch the lives of a very poor or destitute person this year in some creative and personal way.

The Anawim of God

"Yahweh has delivered the soul of the needy from the hands of evil people." (Jeremiah 20:13)

ॐ   ॐ   ॐ

They are:

—the prime victims of environmental degradation and the least to benefit from the pillage of the Earth which brings on such misery;

—absolutely necessary as agents of change to be the backbone on which renewal processes will occur. Their freshness and creativity is required for the quality of the final product;

—needed lest the work does not have the democratic character required for meaningful Earth renewal;

—a stumbling block because their continued poverty is a blight on the Earth. If their wounds are not healed, no true healing will occur.

—God's favorite ones and their clear cry for justice is heard in Heaven.

Action

Within your action group, talk over how each member views the "poor." Do some think the poor bring their condition on themselves? Is there a lingering patronizing attitude among some? How about working together one day a month at a soup kitchen or similar project?

First Stage of Awareness—Come and See

"'Where do you live?,' 'Come and see' he replied." (John 1:38)

      ᥣ   ᥣ   ᥣ

In "World Watch," Spring, 1990, Alan B. Durning states that "More than 200 million people have joined the ranks of the poor since 1980," and this has reversed a 30-year downward trend. These people are caught in a "poverty trap" that includes environmental degradation, external debt, population growth and inequitable development policies. The richest billion people earn 20 times as much as the poorest and use many times as much resources. Without major changes, poverty will continue to rise—and so will environmental degradation.

Ecotourists are spectators demanding to see so they can be saved. They watch horrors on television news programs and are afraid to be caught standing idly by. Omission is a terrible wrongdoing. The big Judgment Day question haunts those of us with filled bellies who know too little and possess too much. Let's go out and see the poor we read about. It's reasonable to become eco-tourists. It's worth a vacation trip, will make us appreciate what we have, will offer us a meaningful experience, and give us something to chat about.

Action

Return demeaning tourist literature depicting the plight of lower income people to the sender with an explanation of why it offends you.

Ecotourism has its Flaws

"Lord, when did we see you a stranger and make you welcome, naked and clothe you, sick or in prison and go to see you?" (Matthew 25:38-39)

                      ᒫ   ᒫ   ᒫ

What about the poor ones on the receiving end of ecotourism? Demeaned? Exploited? Is it an incendiary situation? An exercise of the elite? Why expend time to entertain the observers? They require fuel and resources to come and see us, and they take our uncompensated time in their self-righteous learning process. Antarctica's growing field of ecotourists are threatening to triple in each succeeding year—and trash that pristine continent, all in the name of ecology. In fragile moss, ecotourist footprints are the same as those of developers. Each will last a century.

Action

Engage someone who wishes merely to see poorer living conditions to do something more and work for Habitat for Humanity.

Second Stage of Awareness—
Come and Give

*"If one of the brothers or sisters is in need of
clothes and has not enough food to live on,
and one of you says to them, 'I wish you well;
keep yourself warm and eat plenty,' without
giving them these bare necessities of life, then
what good is that?"* (James 2:15-16)

ɞ   ɞ   ɞ

Ecotourism's limitations make one move from being
mere spectator to actor or doer, trying to make right an
injustice in our world. There's much good in volunteering, for only in giving do we receive. The giver becomes
enthusiastic, sees self-worth, realizes poverty on site, is
appreciated by many.

But giving entails risks. Charitable givers have to overcome their own self-importance, appreciate the gifts of receivers of their largesse, see that self-interest mixes easily
with pity, a better-than-thou attitude, and a condescending
and patronizing manner. Receivers can lose self-esteem
through a heavy dose of charity. Can't an ideal volunteering
be geared to allowing receivers to do things for themselves?

Action

Give to charity, not out of a sense of power but humbly
recognizing that our giving is from God's generosity to
us.

Questions for the Ecovolunteer

*"Let me have no more of the din of your chanting, no more of your strumming on harps.
But let justice flow like water, and integrity like an unfailing stream."* (Amos 5:23-24)

ха   ха   ха

—Why is it better to come and give when you have so many problems at home?

—Is your gift really in earnest or is it a subtle power trip through which you effect changes which you, not we, desire?

—This is not a matter of your giving, but of our refraining from taking what is rightly ours. Why do you give what is really someone else's? Is it for fear that we will rise up and take?

—If you must give and we must take, why not give us the means to allow us to do the same work ourselves?

—Why give if this is not going to be appreciated?

—Is giving a mere way to feel better, or do all activities contain mixed motives?

Action

Search out with another answers to these questions. It is wise to do this in company with lower income people, and possibly the recipients of your charity.

Third Stage of Awareness—
Come and Be With

"So if all that we have in common means any-
thing to you, welcome him as you would me;
but if he has wronged you in any way or owes
you anything, then let me pay for it." (Philemon 17-18)

୫   ୫   ୫

The Earth beckons us to be partners, cooperators, those who are with the poor, public participators, mutual givers and receivers, not working for others but with them. Really, can the middle class do any more than work with people? We cannot become poor except in Spirit, and with this chasm always present we tend to make the best of it. Our very difference is part of our own special poverty. In our differences we still find grounds in which to cooperate and work out salvation together.

While this is a great advancement over the levels of ecotourist and ecovolunteer, ecopartnership is not perfect. There is a distance which is as real as we allow it to be. Those who are middle class have condemned themselves to a way of thinking, a way of life from which they are chained and cannot be liberated. Part of our journeying to deeper levels is seeing the weakness inherent in the "we" and "they," the lack of identity with the poor. At its most honest moment the lurking question is whether "we" really want to be identified with the "they."

Action

Find a way of doing things with lower income people, such as helping them repair or insulate their homes. Reflect on the motive involved. Do you seek deeper connectedness?

TODAY WE KNOW
WHAT THE NEW TESTAMENT
ALWAYS KNEW-THAT MIRACLES
ARE SIGNS POINTING TO THE
PRESENCE OF A DIVINE POWER
IN NATURE AND HISTORY AND
THAT THEY ARE IN NO WAY
NEGATIONS OF NATURAL LAWS

Fourth Stage—Come and Be

"Set up signposts,
raise landmarks;
mark the road well,
the way by which you went.
Come home, virgin of Israel,
come home to these towns of yours."
(Jeremiah 31:21)

        ❧   *❧*   *❧*

We are part of the community of all beings on Earth and hold an ongoing relationship with them. Both our origin and destiny are tied to that of other earthly creatures. What we ultimately strive to do is ensure our oneness with them. Affirming this relationship allows us to move towards identification with that Earth community. Identification cements community and community gives identity. Now we can say "we" and not "they" when referring to the poor. It is not because poverty is a goal to achieve, but because the poor ones are so precious, privileged, necessary, and present that we cannot in love or justice remain apart. We are empowered by embracing the paradox of the powerlessness of the poor. And this discovery is truly enriching.

Action

Consider an alternative vacation living among poor folks while paying for your own upkeep. Enter into their joys and sufferings.

Power of Presence

"I am the vine,
you are the branches.
Whoever remains in me, with me in him,
bears fruit in plenty;
for cut off from me you can do nothing."
(John 15:5)

         ᶚ   ᶚ   ᶚ

Earth lovers realize that many of their goals may not be reached immediately and that success will be illusive. To paraphrase Mother Teresa, isn't it better to be faithful rather than successful? In working with the poor, we discover a new fidelity that keeps us going even when the poverty seems endless and anticipated results appear never to come. Keeping the lamps of hope burning is itself a faithful act, and in some strange way allows an opening for success—but not as the world views it.

This new revelation is being down-to-Earth. Within the powerlessness of the lowly we find ourselves in the nakedness of being anew, different, willing to penetrate where others turn away. We are present to and with them and their presence becomes a communion and identification. Success is no longer of value and its delay will not disturb us. We will win because we have won already. It is not merely gaining quality points for heaven. Rather presence is an energy-building unity, a burning love wrapping us together.

Action

Create a meeting opportunity where people will hear the testimony of someone who is truly present with the poor.

The Poor Are the Key

"For the least among you all, that is the one who is great." (Luke 9:48b)

ॐ　　　　　　ॐ　　　　　　ॐ

The preferential option for the poor is to see God's deep wish to always stand by the little ones, the forgotten, the overlooked. It is fairness overflowing, a desire that the goodness of all creation be shared and realized by us as by One who loves all. The poor are our key to our own becoming, if we are willing to open ourselves to them. Then we become small so that all might become great.

Ecologically, this mysterious hidden power is found in doing very natural and down-to-Earth operations, in preferring a suitable or appropriate technology which limits resource use, in "thinking poor" and thus with less demands on the resources of the world, and in choosing those actions and services which are lower on the food and consumer chain of resources. Our offer to be poor is our opening to a vastly higher quality of life.

Action

Plan a small project. Now consider what it would be like with half the resources or a quarter of them. Isn't it best to do it with less? What really is the minimum required to complete the project?

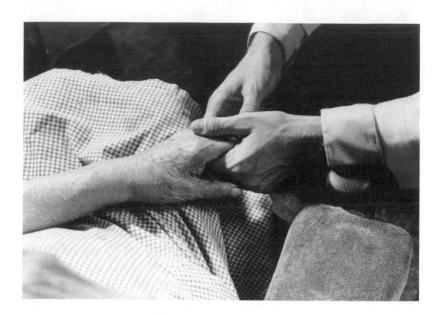

Acceptance of Vulnerability

"Remember, I am sending you out like sheep among wolves; so be cunning as serpents and yet as harmless as doves." (Matthew 10:16)

ঽ৯ ঽ৯ ঽ৯

Being poor is being able to be wounded. We accept the good of the other in such a degree that we are hurt when they hurt. We have a compassion and we suffer when our lowly brothers and sisters do not rise as they should and ought. Standing beside and among those who get hurt so easily, because they are society's prime victims, will open us to being hurt as well. Identification strips off the insulation of security. Being poor says: if you love them you become them, and now you pay the price of being vulnerable and just as insecure.

Vulnerability includes being passed over. The powerful have access to the media and can command publicity. But the poor do not have such privilege without taking very drastic measures. This lack of access sharpens the poor's creativity to find ways of getting around and winning when all odds are against the overlooked and marginated—and that makes us more vulnerable. Poor folks don't change structures from within because we are not part of the power elite. And being on the outside opens us to accusations, arrests, denunciations, and misrepresentations because we are now poor. We can't have it both ways. If not among the poor, we have ways of getting off. Being poor means we must take the extra knocks. It is now our sacred privilege.

Action

Resolve to take some environmental action. Is it best to work within the system or outside of it and why? Spend time talking this over with others and pray over the matter.

Seeking Forgiveness

*"But you do forgive us: and for that we revere
you."* (Psalm 130:4)

ða   ða   ða

Oh, Creator God! Are You offended?
Oh, Creatures of the Earth! Are you suffering?
Oh, Special Places and Times! Are you desecrated?
Oh, Lowly People! Are you tasting toxic water
and breathing foul air
and living in polluted neighborhoods?

For my part in causing these misdeeds to have occurred;
For our participation in the social sin of
environmental degradation;
For neglecting to curb our Earth's
resource depletion;
For failing to stop the culprits who
continue to pollute—
I humbly ask pardon.

Action

Accept God's forgiveness.

IV. Doing First Things First

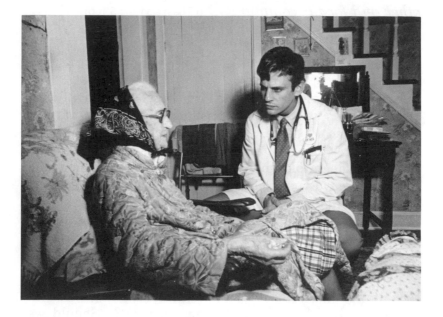

Doing First Things First

*"You must all think of what is best for each
other and for the community."* (I Thessalonians 5:15b)

        ❧   ❧   ❧

Urgency drives us forward to deeper levels of consciousness as we strive to respond to the cry of poor Earth and poor people. We find great numbers of hurting creatures and limited time to give assistance. Conditions become intolerable because globally a trillion dollars each year is used for military weaponry and conflicts which could be spent on ecodefense. A mere tithing of the international military budget would free sufficient funds to check the rapid deterioration of the global environment—but even that is unrealistic to those holding the power in war games rooms.

Is it best to work only with those hurting close at home (thinking globally but acting locally)? Should we focus on environmental problems which have greater chance of public awareness and governmental response? Should we concentrate on healing people and then, if time permits, turn to nonhuman environmental issues? Isn't part of the pain not knowing where to give our immediate attention?

Action

List the five environmental problems which appear most serious in our world. Are there any of these to which you can give some personal or group attention? What are you going to do?

A Temptation

"How much longer must I endure grief in my soul, and sorrow in my heart by day and by night?" (Psalms 13:2a)

          ❧   ❧   ❧

We are tempted to describe our embattled Earth in warfare terms and apply the French World War I practice of "triage" when medical care was limited and casualties great. That consisted of dividing victims in three categories: those most serious being allowed to die; those middling being treated, if time and resources permitted; those most likely to recover being attended. This sorting method is not so outmoded as might seem: it's the current American foreign policy. Namely, the least likely to recover (Fourth World, e.g., Haiti and Sub-Sahel) are given virtually nothing; the Third World gets leftovers; and greatest attention is now given to the Second World which is most likely to recover. How do the forsaken feel?

Action

Read about some "Fourth World" situation such as in Haiti or Bangladesh. Contact a relief agency which is giving technical assistance in any of this class of countries. Offer support in some manner.

The Destitute

"Yahweh, you listen to the wants of the humble,
you bring strength to their hearts,
you grant them a hearing, judging
in favor of the orphaned and exploited,
so that the earthborn may strike fear no
longer." (Psalm 10:17-18)

❧   ❧   ❧

Identification with the poor (who may range from pensioners and unemployed to low income and homeless) does not mean that we become destitute. Destitution is a very poor quality of life and no one aspires to imitate that burden, that privation of life. All need proper food, health care and rest. The destitute can hardly assist fellow human beings in great need due to their own condition and lack of time for reflection, a necessary ingredient for environmental action. Hopefully, destitution is a temporary condition, and triggers our heartfelt response. It exists in the Sub-Sahel, in Asian refugee camps, and in Latin American barrios.

Extreme poverty and severe environmental degradation are two sides of the same coin which plagues our planet. Ignoring destitute people means not comprehending destitute Earth. The Earth's desolation makes it rootless, devoid of its own healing power, thrown at our mercy. How do we respond?

Action

Plan a session of your reflection group on ways to face and confront destitution. Discuss the possibility of conversion of resources from military to ecodefense. How can others exert influence on this matter?

The Poor Will Rise

"The hungry God has filled with good things . . ."
(Luke 1:53a)

૨ૡ   ૨ૡ   ૨ૡ

The environmentally concerned's hope is that the poor will rise up and enjoy a reasonable quality of life and not covet excessive wealth. A good quality of life includes adequate food, clean water, proper shelter, clothing, health care, and education and time for personal development. A precondition to elevating the poor is to bring the destitute to a level of self-sufficiency where they can become partners in the ongoing struggle. But can this development occur while respecting the dignity of all the persons involved? Will such an undertaking be by their own power, or through the largesse of those now empowered, or by the combination of both?

The participation of the poor is essential, and of all parties (haves and have-nots) is ideal. Isn't it better to enter into a giving-receiving fellowship with those in power so that both give and both receive simultaneously—a mutual sharing of resources? Ideally yes. Does realism include a dream that this is possible?

Action

Give a talk in a local elementary or high school on the problem of the "have-nots" of this world and their current condition. Allow students to vent their views and challenge them on what they can do.

The Affluent Will Be Brought Low

"The rich he sent empty away." (Luke 1:53b)

꙳   ꙳   ꙳

A better world requires radical change. The rising of the poor and the simplifying of the affluent may go hand in hand, so that all meet on a plateau of equality. An ideal hope; a wishful thought; a utopian dream. One movement upward would obtain the minimal amount needed for decent human living; the other movement from extravagance and wasteful living includes the design of a higher quality of life at lower consumption levels. Will it work? Most likely not, for the affluent class fail to understand the ravages of material addiction and how it cripples one's will power. Could it possibly happen? If we say it could with enough conviction, it might.

Action

Go to a bible study group and discuss the social sin of overaffluence. What did the various prophets say on this subject? Are these words relevant to our nation and its current condition?

"A Gift to be Simple"

Simplification leads to:

—fewer waste products and less demands on the natural resources of the Earth (affluent people use on an average 20 times the resource expenditure of the poor). By reducing meat consumption or transferring to a meatless economy, we could return some of the 200 to 250 million acres of U.S. meat production land to woodlands and native prairie. Corn or wheat provide 22 times more protein than feedlot beef per calorie of fossil fuel consumed and soybeans are 40 times more efficient.

—reduced pressure to maintain and secure products. Much of the Western military conflict in the Middle East is due to a demand for oil to make or fuel frivolous products and services;

—less demand for higher income. There is almost as much stress-related illness in this country (heart attacks, ulcers, etc.) due to affluence as is attributable to poverty;

—converting saved resources to more cultural and quality of life pursuits. Through a simpler approach we can perceive nature more clearly, meditate more deeply, and become free from peer pressure demands.

—decrease in food excess intake (large amounts of red meat and fats) and improved health.

—a more gentle approach to all within the Earth community. Blatant affluence is harsh; it silences the just demands by future generations for their fair share of basic materials on this limited Earth.

Action

Discuss these points with your reflection group. Do all agree? Consider reducing consumption of resource-intensive food products, such as red meat and overly-processed food items.

Renunciation: Ideal Simplification

"Remember how generous the Lord Jesus was:
he was rich, but he became poor for your
sake, to make you rich out of his poverty."
(2 Corinthians 8:9)

❧   ❧   ❧

Many argue convincingly of the powerful and spiritually-energizing choice of voluntary simplicity, which allows otherwise unnecessarily-consumed resources to be shared by others. A few have always led the way and done just this, e.g., St. Francis, Thoreau, Gandhi. The problem is not in the voluntary renunciation but in the small number of those willing to do this, especially in a consumer-addicted society. And the sheer numbers of addicts can overwhelm the system.

Realism includes much so-called change as fads, a few cases of individual heroics, and the lethargy of the large numbers. The lifestyle change needed would exceed the groundswell akin to the advent of the Peace Corps in the early 1960s. After two decades working for voluntary simplicity, this author has seen little movement toward that change. Yes, some noble souls have done so, but these were generally not consumer addicts. Realism says it won't happen without a miracle, and wise policy is not based on expected miracles.

Action

Introduce in group conversation the subject of how you have changed your lifestyle for the better through using less resources. Show others that growth in quality of life does not mean increased consumption of energy or materials.

Regulation: Enforced Simplification

"The one who loves discipline, loves knowledge;
stupid is the one who hates correction."
(Proverbs 12:1)

&a;   &a;   &a;

Gradualism is an option for action: a combination of carrots (enticements) and sticks (public regulations). This implies a more orderly transition from powerful to powerless. For every regulation there are people who can hire lawyers to get around it. Regulations are slow to be instituted and are often applied in an unfair manner. The poor have less of a chance to influence regulations than do the powerful. Our economic system affords the legal status of "person" with no corresponding responsibilities to corporations existing to increase product consumption. Expect a fierce fight if consumer products are strictly regulated by sticks. Furthermore, consumer addicts find carrots distasteful and the government can't afford them either.

Action

Write (or urge those who never have written to write) to your congressperson and ask for speeding the timetable for more efficient automobiles. Ask why there should be average auto efficiencies and why there shouldn't be a minimum miles/gallon for ALL domestically-manufactured or imported cars.

Economic Downturn: Simplification in Hard Times

"For nation will fight against nation, and kingdom against kingdom. There will be earthquakes here and there; there will be famines. This is the beginning of the birthpangs." (Mark 13:8)

ح‌ه ح‌ه ح‌ه

A complete breakdown in the economic system through external or internal factors may force affluent high rollers to discontinue their consumptive patterns. A major depression would stop many yacht engines—at least for awhile. One cannot hope for such a catastrophe or plan it as an orderly change of events. Some economists predict that sooner or later a major collapse may come, and then major readjustments in the consumer culture will have to be made. However, history shows that economic downturns often affect the poor more than the affluent, and so these episodes seldom produce an equality of lifestyle, only one of decreased expectations. Many who endure such crises do not permanently change lifestyle, only suppress practices during an unfavorable period.

Action

Discuss with your reflection group about who truly suffers in hard times. Ask older persons who endured the Great Depression to participate. What were lessons to be relearned now?

Frustration: Terrorist Simplification

*"He will do that by the same power with
which he can subdue the whole universe."*
(Philippians 3:21)

        ða.   ða.   ða.

This approach resembles hostage-taking in various parts
of the world. Doing something illegal, which cannot be easily penalized, allows the powerless to frustrate the smooth
operation of complex systems of the powerful. Affluence (sophisticated transportation systems, urban life, rapid transfer
of people and goods) is increasingly complicated and thus
more exposed to such acts of sabotage. The violent poor
aren't stupid; they sense power and are willing to grab for it.
They realize that the networks sustaining affluence are increasingly vulnerable to attack by modern guerrillas—and
they are becoming increasingly desperate. The likelihood is
that it will be this form of attack that will bring down the
excess consumption habits of many. Some say it follows a
pattern akin to the decline of the Roman Empire.

Action

Write your own reflections on the Ecoterrorism which
resulted during the Gulf War. Was our thirst for cheap
foreign oil partly to blame? Are we more vulnerable for
not being self-sustaining in such basic bulk materials
like our fuel? Advocate for the return of solar tax credits
to encourage local, safe, renewable, environmentally-benign energy sources.

Revolution: Bottoms-Up Simplification

"Your mind must be renewed by a spiritual revolution so that you can put on the new self that has been created in God's way, in the goodness and holiness of the truth."
(Ephesians 4:23-24)

እ።   እ።   እ።

Turning the tables upside down could allow the lowly to take what is rightly theirs (and run the risk of becoming like the original oppressor in the process). People who abhor such a happening quickly mention that the poor have no guarantee of doing any better, and that through force they may become the oppressors. However, affluence is no guarantee of benevolent action, as history has already proven. Revolution is a part of human history, the violent turning out of office of those in power. It occurs at least once each year somewhere in the world. The dynamics of revolution continue to work so that the outs become ins and ins, outs. Making a better life is unpredictable.

Action

Radicalize your own thinking by becoming more self-sustaining in food, fuel, building materials and water. Think and develop the possibility of home gardening, solar energy, rammed earth construction, and a cistern to collect water.

The Launching Time

*"There is a season for everything, a time for
every occupation under heaven. . . ."*
(Ecclesiastes 3:1)

૭ა   ૭ა   ૭ა

—when pollution is life-threatening. We need to act when
a polluter contaminates a domestic water source with a
toxic material. People develop cancer. Animals and plants
are poisoned. Remedial action is called forth. If the water
source cannot be immediately cleaned, then we should help
develop and find alternative sources of domestic water, such
as the construction of cisterns.

—when large numbers are affected. The destruction of
Antarctica's ecosystem by the depletion of the ozone layer is
serious. While the affected human population is a few
thousand people at any given time, relatively large numbers
of penguins and other animals are present. Many mam-
mals in proximity of the continent will be affected by the
destruction of their marine food chain—the small
shrimplike malacostracan crustaceans called "krill."

—when environmental conditions are hard to control. Nuclear wastes are lethal for tens of thousands of years, making it imperative to ask whether the wastes should be toler-
ated in the first place—especially if the electricity produced
by nuclear power generation is used for frivolous pursuits.

Action

Apply pressure to have aging nuclear power plants
decommissioned in an environmentally-safe manner.

A Call for Added Trust and Joy

"O soil, do not be afraid; be glad, rejoice, for Yahweh has done great things. Beasts of the field, do not be afraid; the pastures on the heath are green again . . ."
(Joel 2:21-22a)

         ه   ه   ه

Part of a down-to-Earth philosophy is not to let urgent times paralyze us. Some are tranquilized by the bad news and find it impossible to move forward. Priority-setting requires us to see through the gloom and continue with hearts of joy. Conquering fear leads to contagious trust, just as the fear of things to come can infest all of creation and force it in upon itself.

Action

Have an "Earth Party" and celebrate some of the small achievements in the community. Have music and entertainment.

V. Naming Eight Models for Action

Naming Eight Models For Action

"The particular way in which the Spirit is given to each person is for a good purpose." (1 Cor. 12:7)

ર   ર   ર

Much effort is lost among environmental groups by squabbling over approaches and methods for Earth-saving action. Often, more articulate individuals champion one model as the only one. Rather than resolving these battles in favor of a particular action model, what about championing both biodiversity and ecoactivistic diversity? The complementarity of different models working together in teamwork imitates the patterns of both natural systems at work and the manner in which science research teams function. Tolerance and encouragement of our diverse ways of action manifests the Spirit working in our lives towards the rebuilding of the Earth. We honor our diversity which gives a personal touch to whatever level of consciousness we find ourselves.

Depending on our talents, personalities, and the local circumstances at given times, we are drawn to act in different Earth-saving ways. There are at least eight models of environmental action which resemble groups of characteristics found in modern standard psychological and personality types. Though attempting to show the predominant traits of each model might prove fruitful, it awaits further study. What is affirmed is that these different models actually exist today within the environmental movement, and it is enough to describe them and invite others to find their bright and shadow sides. Perhaps further exploration may discover that one or other model is more needed at a given time or place. So be it.

Action

Practice ecological ecumenism. Ask the more searching questions as to whether you hold some environmental practices to be of lesser importance than others or even that some should be prohibited or openly discouraged. Find the good in a variety of actions and publicize it in a positive manner. Pray for the work of others.

1. Mastery Model: Earth as Controllable

"God blessed them, saying to them, 'Be fruitful, multiply, fill the earth and conquer it. Be masters of the fish of the sea, the birds of heaven and all living animals of the earth.'" (Genesis 1: 28)

ᙇ　　　　　　ᙇ　　　　　　ᙇ

Perceiving Earth as unchartered, foreign, removed, and fearsome opens it to being mastered or controlled. Geographic and scientific exploratory achievements have occurred over the past 500 years. Harm resulted when exploration became exploitation (the word is synonymous in several Latin languages) and much resource depletion and pollution of the Earth is traced to false ideas of controlling Earth and mastering resources. Still the human drive for success and achievement produces good effects. Seeing the unknown as the uncontrolled invites scientific inquiry; realizing that this conquest could be done by ever more sophisticated human tools encourages modern technology. Better and more complex communication and transportation systems bring human beings closer together and make the Earth's plight far better known to a global audience.

This mastery model dominates Western thinking even now, draws support and presumed blessings from the Judeo-Christian tradition, and regards mishaps or environmental misdeeds as mere lapses on the road to higher success. Mastery is a challenge which extends often beyond one's own inadequacies to Earth and the subjugation of other people. Mastery proponents may include business people searching for "green products," politicans and office-seekers, money raisers, ecolobbyists, and environmental lawyers. These are organized, champion good management practices, have a drive for success, and try to please their constituents. They can become obsessed with their perceived power.

Action

Master ourselves through self-discipline. Resolve to see all creatures as good in themselves and not just as good for us. Limit our use of material resources to only what is needed.

2. Partner Model: Earth as Mother

"Here is the sign of the Covenant I make between myself and you and every living creature with you for all generations. I set my bow in the clouds and it shall be a sign of the Covenant between me and the earth." (Genesis 9:12-13)

᪐   ᪐   ᪐

A philosophical model espoused by deep ecologists and others follows primitive practices of relating to Earth as partner, substratum and center of our creative process. We are part of an Earth community, spring from it, are not superior to it or dominating it. Other creatures are part of this community and we need to be cooperative and supportive. This model has current popularity as expressed in Creation-Centered Spirituality, Earth consciousness, Gaia Hypothesis proponents, and New Age activities. Contented, easy-going and serene people are comfortable here and include those drawn to spirituality, "Peace and Justice" advocates, libertarians, the Rainbow Gathering folks, homesteaders, hippies, some academics, those attracted to esoteric philosophies, and young people who want to break loose. However, this group needs a down-to-Earth approach and to reflect on the need for an ecojustice stance.

Action

Hug a tree or kiss our mother the Earth.

3. Caretaker Model: Earth as Gift from God

"What sort of servant, then, is faithful and wise enough for the master to place over the household to give them their food at the proper time?" (Matthew 24:45)

&ea; &ea; &ea;

Do we cherish our Earth gift and are we responsible free agents capable of improving or spoiling it? Our lifespan for improving the fragile Earth is short and our harmful practices only borrow from the future generations. Should we be respectful people—stewards—moving lightly on this planet and leaving Earth a better place than when we came? Or will we squander our birthright through wasteful resource consumption? Earth stewards include soil and wildlife conservationists, farmers and agronomists, caretakers of public areas, Nature Conservancy people, tour guides, foresters and tree planters, and others who care for the Earth's resources. They see obedience and loyalty as the highest virtues, but may fail to ask critical questions about where the gifts have come from or whether they should retain them for their own private care and use.

Action

With friends and colleagues, reexamine your attitude toward God-given gifts. How do we use, refuse or alienate them?

4. Good Samaritan Model: Earth as Victim and Harmed

"And who is my neighbor?" (Luke 10:29)

ه   ه   ه

People and other creatures are neighbors, victimized by poor environmental practices. Some solicitous people recognize victims of environmental degradation, immediately help them and show compassion for their plight, and attempt to do something about it. This person is affected by a toxic dump site; this bird is covered with spilled oil; this field is eroding. Good Sams don't like to merely talk; they prefer concrete deeds which enable others to improve. The category includes appropriate technologists, health providers, retired folks, homemakers, or even governmental employees working for regulatory agencies directed at curbing pollution, improving community relations, cleaning up toxic dumps, or feeding the hungry. However, there is a dark side: sometimes Good Sams don't know when they are no longer needed, especially when others could do the work. They should let go.

Action

Set up a water, road, forestry, or other form of monitoring of public property. Report or do something about harmful practices.

TUNDRA PROTECTION AREA

Hundreds of feet cause damage that
takes hundreds of years to restore.

PLEASE STAY ON THE TRAIL!

5. Suffering Servant Model: Earth as Community of Sufferers

"By his suffering shall my servant justify many, taking their faults on himself."
(Isaiah 53:11)

ð   ð   ð

People find value when joining the community of the suffering of the Earth, and becoming witnesses and facilitators of the meaning of suffering itself. In and through cosuffering we become humble servants to plants and animals and to the Earth itself. Such "servants" may transcend their own locality and include a more global perspective. Gravitating to this category are victims of environmental abuse who regard their own suffering as redemptive, the elderly and disabled, those who develop keen observational skills in severely-impacted areas, contemplatives, and people who are un- or underemployed, and the incarcerated. These are pained when others mistreat the environment and squander their own energy, time and resources in a meaningless manner. They are sensitive persons who feel misunderstood and often suffer from mental anguish—which can become their shadow side. Through the servants' faith, the lives of the suffering can be seen as truly important, even when the world's sleek and learned disregard their profound worth as Earth healers.

Action

Persuade shut-ins to pray for Earth-saving activists. Encourage them from time to time and tell them how their prayers are most important for saving our Earth. Defend their high quality of life.

6. Educator Model: Earth as Mystery

"Wisdom is bright, and does not grow dim.
By those who love her she is readily seen, and
found by those who look for her." (Wisdom 6:12-13)

છે.   છે.   છે.

Environmental educators are numerous, enthusiastic, devoted, disciplined, and know how to organize complex technical materials. They are the training personnel for a new Earth-concerned generation. Environmentally-concerned educators sponsor and encourage students to engage in ecovoluteerism, which is becoming quite popular in progressive educational circles (numerous schools require voluntary social work as a prerequisite to graduation). Educators, who work with the poor or environmental victims, can be powerful role models for their students. Besides formal educators, this group includes generators of educational material, educational field testers, researchers, and environmental demonstration workers (e.g., organic gardeners, renewable-energy installers, affordable housing builders). However, care must always be taken because some education is performed in resource-wasteful environments and few are critical of such circumstances.

Action

Create children's environmental materials or support others who desire to do so. Communicate to skilled writers and media people the need for such materials. Try your own hand at environmental storytelling.

7. Prophetic Model: Earth as Oppressed

"Zeal for your house devours me." (Psalm 69:9)

ॐ   ॐ   ॐ

Radical activists using tactics similar to those of the liberation movements of Gandhi's India or Martin Luther King's Afro-Americans see the liberation of other creatures as a continuation of civil rights movements. Activities in this category range from civil disobedience and witnessing to resistance and monkey-wrenching (violence to property and not to people), being precipitated by a violence already done to the Earth and its creatures. Like other models there are wide gradations of involvement; some want to observe or learn (ecotourists), others volunteer in a marginal manner, and a few want to plunge into the battle. Many are assertive, strong-willed, not inclined to follow peer pressure, unorganized, prophetic, impatient, restless. Some regard the radicals as too uncompromising and others see them as harmful to law and order and property—perhaps a shadow side.

Action

Encourage those impelled to take on more radical environmental action so that their acts may be meaningful and properly understood. Caution against violence to other persons.

8. Comic Relief Model: Earth as Whimsical

"We played the pipes for you, and you wouldn't dance." (Matthew 11:17a)

          ða   ða   ða

John Freda, a highly-talented Chicago environmental artist, suggested this model based on the need to not take oneself too seriously. Comic relief in the form of celebration stands in contrast to the environmental crisis and our need to laugh at ourselves occasionally. Light-hearted comics counterbalance serious prophets. The ones who perform this comic service are drawn both by natural inclinations and because of the tension and stress of the times—conditions which are ultimately detrimental to good ecology. This model includes those who see value in another's smile and laugh, the jovial clowns (who may at times forget to be serious), artists, craftspersons, those drawn to lift the heavy-hearted by some form of diversion, poets, musicians, entertainers, and dramatics and liturgical people.

Action

Encourage good environmental art expressions and organize an exhibit or showing in your community. Give special attention to the art of those who have been neglected or are just beginning in their form of environmental activity.

VI. Becoming Willing To Act

Becoming Willing To Act

"This mystery that has now been revealed through the Spirit to the apostles and prophets was unknown to any in past generations."
(Ephesians 3:5)

❧   ❧   ❧

"Let's face it. America is hooked. We are dependent on a daily fix of 17 million barrels of crude oil. Our addiction is so bad that we're ready to wage war—to protect our 'drug of choice' . . ." (Scott Denman, "America's Oil Addiction: The Road to Recovery." Safe Energy Communication Council, 1990.)

The environmental crisis is due in some measure to the lack of knowing, but in major part to the lack of doing—*knowledgable people unwilling to act now.* If that's the crisis, then we need to focus on our individual and collective will power. Are addicted people free to act? Has their will power been weakened? If petroleum and other resource addictions are real, many Americans suffer from debilitating conditions. But all is not lost. There is a way out of addiction through a willingness to use less and to substitute with environmentally-benign alternatives. Seeing one's way out of an addiction is the very first step towards recovery.

Action

Enlist those who have been successful in Alcoholics Anonymous or other Twelve-Step Programs to assist in helping to break the consumer addiction of our nation. Encourage them to lend their expertise and skills in the environmental movement.

Ever Bolder

"Why are you so frightened, you of little faith?"
(Matthew 8:26)

❧   ❧   ❧

Fortitude is not in the genes. No one was born a brave person, though some seem to have the propensity to be reckless, uncaring about personal danger, or afraid of some particular conditions. While fears may hold people back, recklessness has been the scourge of our planet's resources. On the other hand, to admit our consumer addictions takes courage. Fortitude is a divine virtue, but one most generously offered, often refused, and in need of patient cultivation. Being faithful and down-to-Earth about resource use is a good way to grow in courage. Encouraging others to be always caring about resources helps our community fortitude grow as well.

Action

Promote a Natural Resource Day with emphasis on some natural asset in your community. Our center promotes Rockcastle River Day on the first Saturday of June. Others focus on mountains, caves, lakes, wetlands, wilderness areas, or valleys.

The Power of Prayer

*"Ask, and it will be given to you; search, and
you will find; knock, and the door will be
opened to you."* (Luke 11:9)

        ❧   *❧*   *❧*

The secular mind may dismiss prayer. Challenge it.
Secularism has little to offer us in down-to-Earth courage. Just as we must ask for forgiveness from both the
Creator and the created, so we must seek the Creator's—
and created's—help to make us courageous enough to
bear becoming and remaining cocreators. Without prayer
and meditation we will not be open enough to see and
imitate the courageous models all around.

The Earth truly gives us encouragement in its resilience
and fidelity, virtues which we discover only by meditating
within the natural world. We tap into the creating power
through openness to the creative act which surrounds us
and uplifts us in woods and meadows, oceans and mountains. Let's surrender our precious time, and give some of
it up to reflection. Prayer is a courageous deed, for it ad-
mits we can't do things alone. Through prayer we are en-
couraged and empowered to act.

Action

Set aside time each day for prayer. Say a special
prayer for the Earth and its endangered species.

A New Asceticism

"You are the salt of the earth. But if salt be-
comes tasteless, what can make it salty
again? It is good for nothing, and can only
be thrown out to be trampled underfoot."
(Matthew 5: 13)

જ   જ   જ

To act or not to act: that is the question. Certainly every action requires some resources. If we are conservationists at heart we resolve to use practices proven in the past to help usher in the future, namely the New Earth. What appears to be the constant practice of thousands of years of spiritual method (for most world religions) is simple asceticism, or a self-denial for some higher purpose. We exercise our freedom of choice. We refrain from or give up what is a simple, good, but unnecessary material item or service. Ecoasceticism is doing this in order to rebuild our Earth. It is amazing how some young Earth-concerned people are becoming strict in discipline and rediscovering ascetism through not eating meat or eggs or owning automobiles or living in luxurious surroundings. The past haunts and beckons them and draws them to repeat the good practices so that their actions may be more meaningful.

Action

Set aside a time to fast, and observe it.

Auditing Our Current Practices

"None of their members was ever in want, as all those who owned land or houses would sell them, and bring the money from them, to present it to the apostles; it was then distributed to any members who might be in need."
(Acts 4:34-35)

> ❧   ❧   ❧

Down-to-Earth asceticism requires that we realize that others are deeply in need of what are superfluities to those around us and perhaps to ourselves. Only those who know their consumer practices can change them and break their addictions. Do I know what I use in food, clothing, fuel, electricity, personal items, recreation and leisure activities? Do I know what portion of the governmental expenditures on resources goes to my own needs? If I don't, then how do I proceed to curb needless expenditures of limited world resources? Granted, some resource consumption is for others and can be distributed to their resource use rather than credited to us individually. An honest and thorough audit of personal resource becomes a good examination of conscience. We consume more than we think—and when we compare our total with average persons in Third World countries, we see room for asceticism.

Action

Plant trees. Hank Kenney came to the realization that he had used many trees in his long life, and so he spent Earth Day-90 planting the number (350) that he had consumed.

Eco-Diaries

*"Now go and inscribe this on a tablet, write it
in a book, that it may serve in the time to
come as a witness for ever."* (Isaiah 30:8)

        ❧   ❧   ❧

Much of the asceticism of the past did not have limited
natural resources in mind. How much good can I do by
using less resources and energy? Do I live lower on the
food chain this year than last? How else can we become
ascetical and regain will-power except through good conservation practices?

This type of asceticism includes a systematic recording
of our struggles to address questions such as these. It
may be wise to resort to some external diary, for a very
good memory often fades with time. It may be an audio-
tape, a handwritten, typed, or computer-generated
record. Maybe it's cryptic or labored or long-winded or
abbreviated or mere shorthand or straight narrative or
poetic style. Whatever its nature, the record should be
retrievable and accessible for future reference. Resolve
to read it again in the future or write it so others can
read it and profit from it.

Action

Select your record procedure and begin.

Choosing Simple Lifestyle Practices

"I tell you, most solemnly, unless a wheat grain falls on the ground and dies, it remains only a single grain; but if it dies, it yields a rich harvest." (John 12:24)

≥   ≥   ≥

We can't do each and every simple lifestyle practice, and thus must discern which is better now. Without a profound sense of resource conservation and self-denial (e.g., fasting, abstinence, practice of vegetarianism, etc.) no true Earth healing is possible. It all boils down to time-honored, voluntary restraint from use of things which are good in themselves—as is all creation good.

If our limited resources are good, let's share them with others now or the generations to come. The loving manner by which we exercise our simplicity and still achieve our goals is most important. Can we achieve more by using less resources? It is like several congressional candidates who campaign by walking from one end of their district to the other, using far fewer resources than by jetting or driving. Yet, voters are captivated. Through ecoasceticism we can transform our wounded Earth into a healthy place again.

Action

Choose some way to live more simply and make it a project for the year, such as carpooling or installing a solar water heater. Talk to those doing it. Find ways to make it work better. Evaluate the success after a given period of time.

Asceticism and Earth Links

"But in the seventh year the land is to have its rest, a sabbath for Yahweh. You must not sow your field or prune your vine, or harvest your ungathered corn or gather grapes from your untrimmed vine. It is to be a year of rest for the land." (Leviticus 25:4-5)

ॐ   ॐ   ॐ

Is the Earth healed through my asceticism? An overly-individualized asceticism which only sees personal growth and salvation as the issue can be narrow and selfish. The modern ecoascetic is telling us more. The evangelistic saving of the Earth can be linked with our own growth and development through asceticism. Furthermore, we can become spiritually empowered, acknowledging the hypocrisy in our recent practices. We unite ourselves with the world's poor (poor Earth and poor people); we see our faults in a healthy manner and ask the Earth's and Creator's forgiveness; we believe we are forgiven and can move forward; we can become an inspiration for consumer addicts seeking a way out.

Action

Spread the word of what you are doing through newsletter articles, letters to the editor or by calling in to radio programs.

An Annual Life Review

"God, examine me and know my heart, probe me and know my thoughts; make sure I do not follow pernicious ways, and guide me in the way that is everlasting." (Psalm 139: 23-24)

     ಸಿ   ಸಿ   ಸಿ

Growth in ecoasceticism strengthens our will to act. But a key to this growth is a quiet retreat from our routine activities. Naturally, an Earth place is best for Earth-related reviews and decisions. Many find hermitages in the woods or a hiking trail or a summer cabin the perfect place to be. Do it alone or with others as you might find it best.

A review of our own environmental record may include surprises, for we forget much, even our small victories. We may be too hard on ourselves. If there is a pattern of high levels of enthusiasm and then disinterest followed by a new issue of high interest, then we are possibly fumbling. On the other hand we may be stuck on a burdensome issue which is not for us. We may encounter more emotional or psychological concerns than ecological ones—problems of burn out, dislike of others, fear of mistakes, procrastination.

Action

Get out the calendar and fit a retreat into your schedule.

Spiritual Direction

"Better gain wisdom than gold, choose discernment rather than silver." (Proverbs 16:16)

એ   એ   એ

We need to lay our struggles out to others for comment or just acceptance. A facilitator, advisor, environmental consultant, counselor or spiritual director may assist. Sometimes it takes proper feedback from more than a single other person.   Seek advice from those who have been successful in the past with their own asceticism, favoring those who love the   Earth and see their own simple lifestyle as apostolic and evangelistic, i.e., Good News to others.

There are many good ecoadvisors out there who have spent years respecting the Earth and living close to it. Consider the humble and wise. They come from many walks of life, not simply those identified with a special ministry. However, those practiced in spiritual direction may prove of great help, for they can assist us to discover the barriers which stop us from growing more in tune with the Earth and its needs.

Action

Determine to find a spiritual director.

Listing Our Talents

"Now we are seeing a dim reflection in a mirror; but then we shall be seeing face to face. The knowledge that I have now is imperfect; but then I shall know as fully as I am known."
(1 Corinthians 13:12)

         ða   ða   ða

Refining and fine-tuning our Earth-healing actions require thoughtful and prayerful effort. Set aside quality time. Make a record of all the individual (or group) good points and give this some time for reflection. Next, at a different time, list all individual (or group) weaknesses. Take time for any necessary revisions. Allow enough distance between such listings to complete everything. See if those who know us agree with the listing. Construct a profile of the gifts we bring to our Earth-healing activities and the weaknesses which can be compensated for or left unused.

Action

We have unique talents but we are often blind to them. Ask for the strength to discover and use them for the good of the Earth community. Thank God for them.

Decide to Act Now

"The night is almost over, it will be daylight soon—let us give up all the things we prefer to do under the cover of the dark; let us arm ourselves and appear in the light." (Romans 13:12)

❧   ❧   ❧

Decisions take an instant to make but a lifespan to enact. We have made small decisions in the past, but never really large ecological ones. We as an Earth people must decide together that WE CAN SAVE THIS EARTH. Now is the time for that decision, but it involves a collective willpower, for I cannot save this Earth by myself. The time is right when we who have been in a dream world, with visions of utopias which could happen, now see the light of day approaching. Now is the time for the collective will to operate. Will it come about? Let us prove Cassandra's prophecy of Earth's doom false.

Action

Decide to act and do.

Assemble Resources

"All I can say is that I forget the past and I strain ahead for what is still to come."
(Philippians 3:13b)

෨ඁ෨ඁ෨ඁ

For those who are down-to-Earth, the final note must be something practical, not a lone cry to an unheeding world. We help others come to the collective decision by struggling to make our efforts meaningful. St. Francis decided to rebuild a ruined chapel and started out alone. Others soon came and helped—and for that and other great deeds he is called the patron saint of ecology. Dare me to start:

—Human Resources (are there other people in the vicinity who can help? Will they take responsibility and a leadership role when necessary?)

—Physical Resources (does one have access to transportation, copying, telephone or space for operating?)

—Financial Resources (will the activity have sufficient funding opportunities or the potential for money-raising ventures?)

—Informational Resources (proximity to library, government files, universities, research facilities, etc.)

—Media Access (are there some media contacts and possibilities for adequate publicity?) Deliver your message to them in a timely fashion. Have a precise, short, attractive press package. Leave the snake oil at home. Don't either underplay or overplay the situation. Demand audience attention.

Action

Mobilize the available resources.

A Rededication

"Then I saw a new heaven and a new earth."
(Revelation 21:1)

ʔ   ʔ   ʔ

People tell us that we are moved by stories and that in order to redouble our dedication we need new myths—or at least old ones recast to our times. So be it. But let's not look out into the stars but down here to our Earth for the refashioned story. Our model is found among the poor and with our identification with them we can say with one heart: "If only all the poor could have a decent living—proper food, clothing and shelter, proper recreation, education and health, freedom from extinction and wanton exploitation. If only Earth were Eden again."

Our down-to-Earth dream is that this is possible, that we can experience rebirth and that hope will spring eternal. If we are not pie-in-the-sky folks, then let's make the great desire of the poor come true—for mother Earth is capable of nurturing such a dream. However, we must confront the disbelievers who don't want us to talk this way, lest we challenge their privileges. For them our looking to the poor to rediscover this motivation is a betrayal of their social order. We disrupt their patterns, we draw attention to the poor, we upset this present world order, we even utter the unspeakable—that Earth can become a new and greater Eden.

Students can make a difference!

Ecology Student Action Guides
A Program for Developing Global Citizenship

Students care a great deal about the Earth, but don't always know what to do. *Ecology Student Action Guides* are action-oriented resources for high school and middle school students that can help them recognize and begin to deal with environmental issues.

Ecology Student Action Guides are focused sets of experiences, stories, ideas and resources arranged around a series of projects designed to be used by students and teachers. *Ecology Student Action Guides* will:

- guide students as they learn to be independent thinkers.
- prepare students to live more gently on the Earth as individuals.
- show students how to act as a group on behalf of the environment.
- help young people increase their respect for the Earth and all creatures.
- facilitate brainstorming and thinking.
- help students internalize concepts relevant to new environmental demands.
- guide students into new levels of understanding needed to move them into action.

Using these *Guides,* students and teachers will explore the following topics:

- Rainforests
- Animals
- Ambassadors
- Lifestyles
- Wilderness
- Waste and Recycling
- Gardens
- Environmental Model

Titles may be purchased separately or in complete sets of all eight topics.

For more information about *Ecology Student Action Guides,* call or write:

Sheed & Ward
P.O. Box 419492-B
Kansas City, MO 64141
1-800-333-7373

DATE DUE